Ron

love from Mom + Dad

Mar. 27, 1976.

"Happy Birthday".

A
CARICATURE HISTORY
OF
CANADIAN POLITICS

Yours truly

J. W. Sweezoufk.

A

CARICATURE HISTORY

OF

CANADIAN POLITICS.

EVENTS FROM THE UNION OF 1841, AS

ILLUSTRATED BY CARTOONS

FROM "GRIP," AND VARIOUS OTHER SOURCES.

By J. W. BENGOUGH,

WITH AN INTRODUCTION BY REV. PRINCIPAL GRANT, D.D.,

OF QUEEN'S UNIVERSITY, KINGSTON.

TORONTO:
PRINTED AND PUBLISHED BY THE GRIP PRINTING AND PUBLISHING CO.
1886.
1974 Edition: selected from the original
New Introduction by Doug Fetherling
Peter Martin Associates Limited

Entered according to Act of Parliament of Canada, in the year one thousand eight hundred and eighty-six, by THE GRIP PRINTING AND PUBLISHING
Company, Toronto, in the Office of the Minister of Agriculture.

ISBN 0-88778-081-4

Printed in Canada by Web Offset Publications Ltd.

Peter Martin Associates Limited, 35 Britain Street, Toronto M5A 1R7

Introduction to the 1974 Edition

When John Wilson Bengough died in Toronto in 1923, John Diefenbaker was an apprentice lawyer little known outside Prince Albert, and this is one of the small pities of Canadian history. It deprived us of the opportunity of seeing how Diefenbaker—with his wattles and Dylan Thomas bug-eyes, the caricaturist's dream—would have been rendered by the great pioneer political cartoonist of a nation always distinguished for its graphic wits. As it was, Bengough had to content himself with Sir John A. Macdonald, and the image he created of that lanky head of state with varicose nose and vulpine cleverness is the one that survives most commonly today. Since the life of *Grip,* the magazine Bengough founded and in which he published most of his work, coincided roughly with Macdonald's political life, the two are inextricably mixed. Time and again the cartoonist satirized the Prime Minister in his visual editorials until at last Macdonald seemed to become one of those symbols, like Liberty, John Bull and Uncle Sam, which cartoonists use as a kind of shorthand.

But don't think Bengough was harassing beyond good taste the architect of Confederation when you view the sometimes malicious drawings which follow. It is merely that these cartoons—selected from Bengough's two-volume *Caricature History of Canadian Politics,* published in 1886— cover in the sly fashion of the time a wide range of issues, many of which involved Macdonald. Despite the artist's prefatory notes on each, however, many of the topics he commented on in the original compilation are obscure today. (These have been omitted from this one-volume selection.) It is testament, however, to the pointedness of Bengough's style as well as to the continuity of history, that many of the others are still alive and as hotly debated now as a century ago. Here you will see cartoons on such familiar themes as nationalism, feminism, corruption, Senate reform and that old standby, provincial rights. It was Bengough's cartoons on another hardy perennial, the Canadian Pacific Railway, which first brought him wide acclaim and made him a political force.

Bengough was only twenty-two when he founded *Grip.* He was born in Toronto in 1851 of a Scots father and Irish mother and of his four siblings two ended up in government, one in business and the other became an artist in New York. The family lived in the town of Whitby, near Toronto, and after finishing school there Bengough worked in a local law office. Like a surprising number of other writers before and since, he decided that the legal profession did not suit his temperament and so became a printer's devil at the local newspaper, which was small enough to allow him to discover his latent talent as reporter and cartoonist. At twenty he moved to the city and went to work at George Brown's *Globe,* the most influential paper in the land. But the young Bengough soon found his ego and talents constrained on a publication so dominated by Brown's personality and political style, and in 1873 he started the weekly *Grip* (named for the raven in Dickens' *Barnaby Rudge*). He wrote and illustrated it himself for the most part and treated all current views with healthy disrespect, except those he himself championed—the Single Tax, woman's suffrage, laissez-faire economics, antivivisectionism and the prohibition of alcohol and tobacco.

Throughout Bengough's editorship, which lasted until 1892, the magazine was successful once it was able to attract attention to itself. This became possible with Bengough's cartoons on the Pacific Scandal of 1873, in which irregularities in the previous year's election came to light during an investigation of the CPR, and Macdonald's Conservative government was toppled. This was natural material for J.W. Bengough at his best, and his cartoons (such as "The Dainty Dish", reprinted here) caused a furor. It was the turning point for Bengough as a cartoonist. When he died at seventy-two, he was considered something of a grand old man. He had published his own work in both *Grip's Cartoons* (1875) and the *Caricature History* (which includes some earlier cartoons from other sources) and had drawn for no fewer than four papers in London as well. The British editor, W.L. Stead, had called him "one of the ablest cartoonists in the world", and the *New York Herald* had termed him "the greatest cartoonist living on this side of the continent". Thirty years after his death a bronze plaque commemorating him was unveiled in Toronto. He was the second Canadian journalist (the other was Brown's partner Sir John Willison) to be so honoured.

To understand Bengough's work it is necessary to know something of newspapering in his day. Publishing costs were low, unions being almost nonexistent, and newspaper owners had a virtual monopoly on the dissemination of news. On election nights, for example, crowds would clog the streets in front of the many newspaper offices to await the posting, in windows and on rooftops, of returns telegraphed from distant points. Newspapers were a voice to which people listened rather than spoke through, and which sheet they listened to was determined largely by the political party to which they belonged. Publishers were devoted to things other than truth and sometimes held office, as well as the power to actually sway elections through their paper. Libel laws were invoked more often than now, and with more cause—but to less effect. It was an age, antithetical to our own, in which the editorial page meant much and the sports page little. In this scheme of things, a cartoonist like J.W.

Bengough, who could get away with murder by making carnage funny, was an important person indeed.

It was a time also in which technology or the lack of it, rather than the desire for a more visually fetching product, determined what newspapers looked like. Before half-tone photographs became the staple illustration, papers depended upon prolific sketch artists to record scenes or, if necessary, concoct them. Their work was printed by means of line engravings done partly by hand, and if Bengough's work seems a little overwrought by today's standards, it must be remembered that he flourished in a Victorian era when superfluousness in crosshatching, as well as in dress and rhetoric, was normal.

Bengough's style became more intricate as he grew older. The drawings in *Grip's Cartoons* (some of which he used again in the *Caricature History*) tend to be more fluid than his later ones, but no less skilfully conceived in their premises or gag situations. In his time an ability to sketch was something cultivated and frequently used, like good penmanship, and so his panels were really more cartoons than caricatures. He did not exaggerate a subject's features as much as do modern cartoonists, such as Ed Franklin of the *Globe and Mail* (who sometimes resembles Bengough in other ways) or Duncan Macpherson of the *Toronto Star*. Most Canadians of the 1870s and 1880s would not have seen Sir John A. Macdonald, much less his constant photographic image, so Bengough had scant room for licence. Rather, he tried to capture the essence of the man's appearance and to match that with his political nature. It is interesting to note that Bengough's pictures of Macdonald as a middle-aged man show him, rightly, in his prime (Macdonald was fifty-eight when *Grip* began) and that it is only nearer his death, after the election of 1891, that the politician in Bengough's drawings assumes the haggard appearance of the scarecrow W.C. Fields we like to connect with his shade.

Unlike most modern cartoonists, Bengough felt it was necessary to label anything that might be unfamiliar to his less informed readers or to use wordy cutlines and titles. In our time, the editorial cartoon has grown mute except in the school headed by Sid Barron of the *Toronto Star* and Len Norris of the *Vancouver Sun*, who sequester small jokes around the page, much as Bengough often did. What then, if the styles have changed so drastically, if today's cartoonists are strictly speaking much better draughtsmen, is the enduring importance of J.W. Bengough? The answers, I think, lie in three areas.

The first is wit. With Bengough, a picture was figuratively worth ten thousand words and sometimes literally as well. He was cutting and cruel but seldom inaccurate, and with one sketch could apply more weight than a compositor with a verbose editorial in the form of ten pounds of lead type. The second and third areas have to do with what these drawings tell us about Canada and journalism in his time. His sketches give us the sociological, economic and political feel of the first few decades after Confederation. They point out the ways in which we differ from our antecedents as well as the ways in which we resemble them. It is generally the differences that supply the most interest, and Bengough and the others like him are good examples.

He was not merely a cartoonist, as most of our present-day editorial artists are. He was an extraordinary man in a time of extraordinary men, of dilettantes, gifted amateurs and general practitioners who made journalism and society operate in a rather more individualistic manner than today. He was a fighter and campaigner as well as a writer of (by our standards) amazing versatility. In addition to the books of cartoons, he published several volumes of verse illustrated by himself; a political primer for children, similarly adorned; and various other works, including, the year before his death, *Bengough's Chalk Talks,* material from the illustrated lectures which he began delivering a year after his magazine was founded and which brought him fame in Canada, Britain, the United States, Australia and New Zealand. He saw nothing unusual in writing songs, humour, fiction and drama as well as embroiling himself in various economic, literary, academic and political matters. (He withstood urgings to run for Parliament as a Prohibitionist, apparently feeling his independence would be compromised, but served later as a Toronto alderman.) Nor was he unusual for his time in all this. One need look no further than *Grip's* associate editor, Phillips Thompson (Pierre Berton's grandfather), for another example of the same breed. They were great men in a small way, and it is tempting in this book of Bengough's sketches to believe that the greatest cartoonist of his time was dealing with his own superior race of men, linked to us only by history and the basics of human nature. It is certainly human nature that Bengough is dealing with, and it is his understanding of it, as much as his talent, that makes him such a good cartoonist and this such an interesting book.

Doug Fetherling

PREFACE.

"CARICATURE HISTORY" does not mean that history is caricatured. On the contrary, a good caricature enables us to see, in a true light, facts that might otherwise be hidden or misrepresented. We understand current events and the social life of England from the illustrations of *Punch* more truly than from the columns of the *Times* or the *Morning Post*. Canada is only beginning life, and our politics touch subjects of general interest so seldom, that it is sometimes thought and said that there is no field for a Canadian *Punch;* but the fact, perhaps not generally known, that for the last forty years, at any rate, we have rarely been without artists whose pictures on the questions of the day have appealed successfully to popular humor, proves that our political life has been robust from the beginning. Some of these artists had to content themselves with publishing fly-sheets that provoked the laughter of the town, but that had no chance of obtaining more than a local reputation. For others, organs well-known in their day, such as *Punch in Canada, Diogenes*, and *Grinchuckle*, were established at different times prior to 1873, when GRIP vaulted into the seat which he has occupied since to the satisfaction of all Canada. Requests have been frequently made for a work containing a continuous series of his cartoons, and in now acceding to these it has been thought well to give illustrations of what was done among us in the same line previously. Fortunately the publishers were able to obtain selections from the sources to which I have referred, and also from the *Canadian Illustrated News;* and the First Volume of this work thus gives something like a continuous pictorial history of the events that have stirred popular feeling most deeply since 1848. They believe that those older representations will be heartily welcomed, and they desire to thank all who have assisted in making the work so extended.

As to GRIP himself, he needs no letters of commendation, but, with his well-known regard to the established usages of society, he thinks that there should be a Preface to the work. Considering how freely he takes a hand in our concerns, and that, in order to show us what goes on behind the scenes, he has no hesitation in entering bar-rooms, Government Houses, Palaces, and the Privy-Council Chambers of our pastors and masters, this modesty on his part will be duly appreciated by a modesty-loving public.

A young member of our House of Commons waxed eloquent in the course of his maiden speech, and, naturally enough, some of his brethren thought him mad. Not so thought Joseph Howe, to whom Shakespeare was dearer than all the Blue-books in the Parliamentary Library: "Thank God for a bit of poetry in this dry-as-dust House," whispered the old man to a near neighbor. Yes, and thank God for Humor, with its intuitive perception of truth, and its consequent impartiality. Without GRIP, what Saharas our Parliaments would be!

Every man should take an intelligent interest in the political life of his country. But from what quarter is he to get information? He cannot get Hansard; and even if he could, life is too short to read the terrible volumes. To trust himself to this or that party paper will insure interest but not intelligence; and to read the papers on both sides will land him in hopeless scepticism, or drown him "in a popular torrent of lies upon lies." On the whole, he cannot do better than trust GRIP, as the most honest interpreter of current events we happen to have. GRIP, too, not only generally hits the nail on the head, but sometimes hits like a blacksmith—and we belong to a race that loves to see a blow well struck. Besides, the fellow has no malice in him. He has always a merry heart, and that doeth good like a medicine. Many a laugh he has given us, and laughter clears away unwholesome fogs from the spirit. Along with music it is next best to Holy Writ, according to the testimony of Martin Luther. A picture, too, has this unspeakable advantage over verbiage, that you can take in the situation at a glance, and if it is not agreeable, you can pass on. You condemn the representation as unfair, but, at any rate, your time is not lost.

PREFACE.

I do not speak as an artist of the cartoons or the caricatures that illustrate our political history since 1873. To me their artistic merit is exceptionally great, but I am not qualified to speak as a critic of technique. I speak only as a public teacher who knows that the educational influence of pen or pencil may be greater than that of the living voice, and who rejoices when that influence is on the right side.

In this case it is on the right side. GRIP is impartial, in a country where it is very hard to be impartial, and harder still to have your impartiality acknowledged. GRIP is also always patriotic. He is something even better he is healthy. You may think him at times Utopian. You may not agree with the means he proposes, but you must always sympathize with the end he has in view. He is scrupulously clean. He never sneers. In the best sense of the word, he is religious.

One word more: GRIP's humor is his own. It has a flavor of the soil. It is neither English nor American. It is Canadian.

Ladies and Gentlemen, I have the honor formally to introduce to you my esteemed friend, Mr. GRIP. You may receive him with confidence into your homes and hearts.

G. M. Grant

UNIVERSITY OF QUEEN'S COLLEGE,
KINGSTON, *March, 1886.*

DEDICATED

BY SPECIAL PERMISSION

TO

HIS EXCELLENCY THE EARL OF DUFFERIN,

VICEROY OF INDIA, AND FORMERLY GOVERNOR-GENERAL OF CANADA,

DURING WHOSE TERM OF OFFICE " GRIP " MADE HIS FIRST APPEARANCE ; AND TO

WHOSE KINDLY ENCOURAGEMENT " GRIP," IN COMMON WITH CANA-

DIAN ENTERPRISE IN ALL DEPARTMENTS, OWES A

LASTING DEBT OF GRATITUDE.

THE MAN WOT FIRED THE PARLIAMENT HOUSE.

As a climax to the excitement which attended the passage of the Rebellion Losses Bill, the House of Parliament at Montreal was destroyed by incendiarism. This outrage was well known to have been the act of a Party, but the individual hand that wielded the torch, was not known. *Punch in Canada*, the comic paper of the day, and a strong opponent of the measure in question, took advantage of this fact to suggest humorously that "the man wot fired the Parliament House" was Lafontaine—the man who led the Government in the matter which had so excited the Conservative wrath, and so led to the catastrophe.

PUNCH IN CANADA, MAY 19th, 1849.

THE MAN WOT FIRED THE PARLIAMENT HOUSE!

Punch in Canada, 1849.

THE CLUB NATIONALE DEMOCRATIQUE PREPARING TO TRAMPLE ON THE BRITISH LION.

THIS was a satirical allusion to the "tall talk" indulged in by a coterie of French followers of Papineau, who favored a democratic form of Government for Canada as a cure for the prevailing discontent.

PUNCH IN CANADA, JULY 7th, 1849.

THE "CLUB NATIONALE DEMOCRATIQUE,"

PREPARING TO TRAMPLE ON THE BRITISH LION.

Punch in Canada, July, 1849.

THE HERMIT.

LORD ELGIN, the Governor-General, was criticised for secluding himself from society at the official residence, Monklands.

PUNCH IN CANADA, AUGUST, 1849.

THE HERMIT.

Lately discovered in the woods, near Monklands ; and now about to be forwarded to England by
the gentlemen of the British League, to whom this Portrait is respectfully dedicated.

PUNCH IN CANADA, AUGUST, 1849.

DROPPING A HINT.

_____

COLONEL GUGY, M.P., was a prominent member of the Opposition under the Baldwin-Lafontaine Ministry, but announced his withdrawal from that position during the heated scenes which followed the Rebellion Losses riots. He is regarded as having been the progenitor of the Liberal-Conservative Party of the present time. The cartoon conveys the insinuation that Colonel Gugy sympathized with the Annexation movement, which was the sensation of the day.

PUNCH IN CANADA, MAY, 1849.

DROPPING A HINT.

Boy.—Hallo, Mister! ye've dropped yer hankercher.

Leaguer.—Ha! my good boy, yes!—I mean no, my blessed little kid, no! not mine, my excellent little gentleman, not mine—Oh no, no, no, not mine!

Boy.—Well, some o' yis dropped it anyhow, and now none o' yiz 'll own to it.

Punch in Canada, May, 1849.

THE ANNEXATION ENGINE.

THIS was another attack upon the Annexation sentiment which prevailed in
Lower Canada. Mr. Papineau is again the principal figure, and *Punch's*
idea was that if Annexation were ever realized its first effect would be to rob
the French-Canadians of the special privileges they enjoyed under British
rule. The artist's conception of Brother Jonathan is somewhat unique.

PUNCH IN CANADA, 1849.

THE WAY BROTHER JONATHAN WILL ASTONISH THE NATIVES.

ANNEXATION COMES IN BY THE RAIL, WHILE LIBERTY FLIES OFF IN THE SMOKE.

PUNCH IN CANADA, 1849.

THE THIMBLERIG.

THIS cartoon appeared during the discussion of the removal of the Seat of Government from Montreal after the destruction of the old building at the hands of the mob. Hon. Robert Baldwin, who was Premier at the time, was supposed to favor his native place, Toronto, in the selection ; Kingston and Montreal were the other competitors for the honor. Mr. *Punch* naturally gave Montreal the preference.

PUNCH IN CANADA, SEPTEMBER, 1849.

THE GOVERNMENT THIMBLERIG.

Here I am, Sporting Bob from York!—Rowl in here, gentlemen, and stake your money. Now, Mr. Sherwood! I see you looking at one of the thimbles;—walk up, sir, like a man, and go your length upon it in goold or silver,—Debentures taken at a small discount. Here you are, Mr. What-d'ye-call him, the coroner from Kingston! Sport your jinglers here upon the lucky thimble; —a quick eye and a ready observation takes the tin. O, there's the French gentlemen from Montreal feeling for their purses!—step this way, gentlemen, and the day's your own. Rowl in,— *(Here Punch clandestinely tilts up a thimble, and discovers the pea.)*

Punch in Canada, September, 1849.

PAWNING THE FLAG.

MR. BENJAMIN HOLMES was one of the Members for Montreal in the first Parliament after the Union, and was amongst the most active public men of the time. In 1849 he was an advocate of Annexation, and subsequently voted for the reception of an address in favor of Canadian Independence. His Annexation proclivities are hit off in the cartoon, which represents him as pawning the British flag to Brother Jonathan.

PUNCH IN CANADA, OCTOBER 10th, 1849.

LITTLE BEN. HOLMES

AND SOME NAUGHTY CHILDREN ATTEMPT TO PAWN THEIR MOTHER'S POCKET-HANDKERCHIEF, BUT ARE ARRESTED
BY POLICEMAN *PUNCH*, WHO WAS STATIONED "ROUND THE CORNER."

PUNCH IN CANADA, 1849.

THE EAGLE AND THE FAWN.

A piece of excusable self-glorification on the part of Mr. *Punch*, who was " truly loyal " from first to last. Here he dashes forth upon his charger to rescue the Canadian fawn from the talons of the designing American Eagle.

PUNCH IN CANADA, OCTOBER, 1849.

THE EAGLE AND THE FAWN.

PUNCH IN CANADA, OCTOBER, 1849.

TOWNSHIPS COLONIZATION—A SETTLER.

————

THIS was an allusion, from the English standpoint, to the unfitness of French emigrants as agricultural settlers. The contrast between the results of farming industry in Upper and Lower Canada seemed to justify this prejudice. The comparison of the newly-arrived Frenchman to the frogs is a time-honored joke, supposed to have arisen from the alleged French national taste for frogs'-legs as a table delicacy.

PUNCH IN CANADA, 1849.

TOWNSHIPS COLONIZATION—A SETTLER.

YOUNG LITERARY LEADER.—HERE IS ONE SETTLER, SARE, FOR YOUR TOWNSHIP, SARE, ON YOUR FARM, SARE. TOWNSHIPPER.—OH, THAT'S YOUR SETTLER, EH? WHY THERE'S LOTS OF THEM CHAPS HERE ALREADY—IN THE MASHES!

PUNCH IN CANADA, 1849.

A WINTER'S TALE.

AFTER the troubles of 1837, William Lyon Mackenzie became an exile from Canada. In the verses in the legend, he recounts his unhappy experiences in political life to Robert Baldwin, who is figuratively represented as bearing him company. The gallows on the mainland in the distance is a reminder that a price had been set upon Mackenzie's head.

PUNCH IN CANADA, 1849.

WINTER'S TALE.

AUTOLYCUS,   *(A Knavish Peddler)*   -   MR. W. L. MACKENZIE.
CLOWN,   -   -   -   -   -   -   -   - MR. BALDWIN.

AUTOLYCUS.—I see this is the time that the unjust man doth thrive. Sure the gods do this year connive at us, that we may do anything extempore. *(Sings.)*

1837.	1838.	1849.
The daisies were dead on Gallows Hill,—	The hemp-fields waving in the breeze—	But now the lark tra lira sings !
With heigh ! the skulkers behind the rail,—	With hey ! the ravens. O how they croak !	A Navy-islander bold am I ;
O then I thought my pockets to fill !	And the birds that hung from the gallows-trees,	And sympathizers may plume their wings
For the red blood flowed and I robbed the mail.	Might rede me then that it was no joke.	All in the clover as they lie.

CLOWN.—He seems to be of great authority ; close with him, give him gold.

PUNCH IN CANADA, 1849.

CROSS ROADS.

Dr. (now Sir) Chas. Tupper was a warm advocate of Confederation, and did more than any other public man to induce his native Province, Nova Scotia (Acadia), to enter the Union in 1867. Hon. Joseph Howe, a much greater statesman than Tupper, and a man of vast influence, was amongst the opponents of the measure in question, and was suspected of a preference for annexation to the United States. In the cartoon the Province is represented as halting between the two opinions, and the loyal artist takes pains to point out that the advantages are all in the way that leads " to Ottawa."

Diogenes, November 20th, 1868.

CROSS ROADS.

SHALL WE GO TO WASHINGTON FIRST, OR HOWE(E)?

A DOMINION EASTER OFFERING.

SIR GEORGE E. CARTIER had been a member of the Commission sent to England to negotiate for the transfer of the North-West Territory to the Dominion, and the surrender of the rights of the Hudson Bay Company. The successful result of the mission was now announced to Parliament. The conditions agreed upon involved a payment by the Dominion Government of £300,000.

DIOGENES, APRIL 16th, 1869.

A DOMINION EASTER OFFERING.

MISS CANADA.—"THANK YOU, SIR GEORGE! I'VE BEEN WAITING FOR HIM SUCH A LONG TIME! BUT DON'T YOU THINK, AFTER ALL, HE MAY PROVE RATHER TROUBLESOME?"

A PERTINENT QUESTION.

––––––––––

THIS cartoon faithfully reflected the sentiments of the Canadian people on the subject of annexation. While it is still true that there is no general feeling in favor of the change indicated, there is an appreciable absence of the unfriendly feeling toward the United States which was generally cherished at this time.

DIOGENES, JUNE 18th, 1869.

A PERTINENT QUESTION.

MRS. BRITANNIA.—"IS IT POSSIBLE, MY DEAR, THAT YOU HAVE EVER GIVEN YOUR COUSIN JONATHAN ANY ENCOURAGEMENT?"

MISS CANADA.—"ENCOURAGEMENT! CERTAINLY NOT, MAMMA. I HAVE TOLD HIM WE CAN *NEVER* BE UNITED."

"FRIENDS IN COUNCIL;" OR, "IS THE GAME WORTH THE CANDLE?"

THE persons represented in this sketch are Hons. S. L. Tilley, Sir George Cartier and A. T. Galt. The latter gentleman resumed for a brief period the charge of the Finance Department, after the resignation of Hon. John Rose. The financial affairs of the new Dominion were not in the most prosperous condition at the moment.

DIOGENES, AUGUST 27th, 1869.

"FRIENDS IN COUNCIL;" OR, "IS THE GAME WORTH THE CANDLE?"

FORBIDDEN FRUIT.

Mr. L. S. Huntington, M.P. for Shefford (Quebec), had entered public life in 1861, and was chiefly distinguished for decided views in favor of Canadian Independence. He soon came to be looked upon as an annexationist in disguise—a fate which awaits every Canadian public man who avows Independence ideas. The Mr. Chamberlain in the cartoon was a gentleman of local repute.

Diogenes, September 24th, 1869.

FORBIDDEN FRUIT.

H—T—N.—"IT'S A VERY PRETTY PLUM—A VERY PRETTY PLUM, INDEED! ENOUGH TO MAKE ANYBODY'S MOUTH WATER!"

CH—MB—N.—"DON'T YOU WISH YOU MAY GET IT? THAT PLUM WILL TAKE SOME TIME TO RIPEN YET; AND WHEN IT FALLS, I FANCY 'OTHELLO'S OCCUPATION WILL BE GONE!'"

(SEE SPEECH OF MR. CHAMBERLIN AT THE BEDFORD AGRICULTURAL SHOW.)

UNCLE SAM KICKED OUT.

THE anti-annexation sentiment which has always.prevailed in Canada is presented with considerable " force " in this picture.

GRINCHUCKLE, SEPTEMBER 23rd, 1869.

UNCLE SAM KICKED OUT!

YOUNG CANADA.—"WE DON'T WANT YOU HERE."

JOHN BULL.—"THAT'S RIGHT, MY SON. NO MATTER WHAT COMES, AN EMPTY HOUSE IS BETTER THAN SUCH A TENANT AS THAT!"

TOO LATE!

THIS cartoon refers to the selection of Sir Francis Hincks for the post of Finance Minister, in opposition to the claims put forth by the press on behalf of others who were considered to be more entitled to the honor.

DIOGENES, OCTOBER 1st, 1869.

"TOO LATE."

FIRST OLD LADY.—"MY LITTLE BOY IS STRONG AND HEALTHY, AND——"

SECOND DITTO.—"MINE HAS BEEN PRACTISING FOR SOME TIME, AND IS QUITE FIT FOR THE PLACE."

MASTER JOHN.—"IT'S NO USE, MY GOOD WOMAN. THIS BOY THOROUGHLY UNDERSTANDS THE BUSINESS, AND KNOWS ALL THAT WILL BE REQUIRED OF HIM. I CAN'T DO ANYTHING FOR YOU AT PRESENT, BUT I MAY SEND ONE OF YOUR LADS UP WEST BY-AND-BY."

"L'HOMME QUI RIT."

———————

UPON accepting office as Finance Minister in the Dominion Cabinet, Sir Francis Hincks presented himself for election in the constituency of Renfrew, the sitting member, Mr. Rankin, making way for him. Sir Francis had declared that the acceptance of office at this time involved personal sacrifice on his part.

DIOGENES, OCTOBER 22nd, 1869.

"L'HOMME QUI RIT."

————L'astre d'un favori,
Qui se croyait un grand ministre,
Quand de nos maux il avait ri.

—*Béranger.*

SCENE FROM THE COMEDY OF "THE TICKET-OF-LEAVE MAN."

SIR FRANCIS HINCKS had but shortly returned to Canada from the Windward Islands, where he had for several years occupied the position of Governor. The claim that he was making a "personal sacrifice" in accepting office seems to have been too much for *Diogenes*.

DIOGENES, OCTOBER 29th, 1869.

THE COMEDY OF "THE TICKET-OF-LEAVE MAN."

(Adapted to the Ottawa stage.)

MISS CANADA.—" YOU'LL TAKE CARE OF THE MONEY, WON'T YOU? YOU KNOW I'M NOT VERY RICH."

MR. MELTER MOSH.—" O, YESH, MA TEAR, I'LL LOOK AFTER TE MONISH! I'M A HONEST MAN; IF YOU DON'T BELIEVE ME, AX BARBADOES AND DEMARARA. DEY KNOW ME, TEN YEARS."

A MOONLIGHT SCENE ON THE OTTAWA.

THIS is another reference to the selection of Sir Francis Hincks as Finance Minister in preference to the other available candidates for the position.

GRINCHUCKLE, NOVEMBER 4th, 1869.

A MOONLIGHT SCENE ON THE OTTAWA.

GRINCHUCKLE.—"FAITH! IF HE GETS AT IT, THERE WILL BE VERY LITTLE LEFT FOR KING CROW OR ANYONE ELSE."

KING CROW.—"IF SOME OF THESE NORTH RENFREW MEN WOULD ONLY FRIGHTEN HIM AWAY NOW, WOULDN'T THE LIKE OF ME HAVE OUR FILL!"

FROM HALIFAX TO VANCOUVER.

THE project of an all rail route from the Atlantic to the Pacific on Canadian territory had begun to be agitated.   The incredulity attributed to Uncle Sam in the cartoon was fully shared by many more immediately interested. The year 1886, however, saw the feat accomplished.

DIOGENES, NOVEMBER 5th, 1869.

FROM HALIFAX TO VANCOUVER.

MISS CANADA.—"THIS IS WHAT WE WANT, COUSIN JONATHAN. IT WILL GIVE US REAL INDEPENDENCE, AND STOP THE FOOLISH TALK ABOUT ANNEXATION."

JONATHAN.—"WAL, MISS, I GUESS YOU'RE ABOUT RIGHT THAR; BUT I'LL BELIEVE IT WHEN I SEE IT."

MACDOUGALL'S SOLILOQUY.

————————

Hon. William Macdougall was appointed to the Lieut.-Governorship of the North-West Territories on the cession of that country to the Dominion by the Hudson Bay Co. The Half-breed settlers, however, deeming it an infringement of their rights that the country was ceded without their formal consent, opposed Mr. Macdougall's entrance on his arrival. He was obliged to return without enjoying the office he had gone to assume.

Grinchuckle, November 25th, 1869.

MACDOUGALL'S SOLILOQUY.

"THERE IS NOT MUCH FUN IN THIS GAME, BUT A MOVE MUST BE MADE WHEN THE KING IS IN CHECK."

ENOUGH IS AS GOOD AS A FEAST.

THIS was an allusion to the debate which took place on the Nova Scotia "better terms" resolution in the House of Commons. Mr. Blake introduced a motion setting forth the unconstitutionality of the bargain which had been made after the Act of Union, under which Nova Scotia got additional subsidy. Honorable J. S. Macdonald, on the other hand, supported the action of the Government. In connection with this cartoon *Grinchuckle* addressed the following lines to "Joe Howe" :—

> It's of no use, Joe Howe, to be craving for plunder,
>   For we know you are but a political rake ;
> And Ontario will never consent to strike under,
>   While she has for her leader redoubtable Blake.
>
> Old Sandfield, we know, is a premier squeezable,
>   And he's willing to give, and you're eager to take ;
> He would buy up your Province by any means feasible ;
>   But he cannot buy up that redoubtable Blake.

GRINCHUCKLE, DECEMBER 9th, 1869.

ENOUGH IS AS GOOD AS A FEAST.

J. S. M꜀D——LD.—"YES, MY PET, YOU SHALL HAVE IT. I COULD NOT FIND IT IN MY HEART TO DEPRIVE YOU OF IT."

E. BL——E.—"YOUR PET! SHE WAS NOT ALWAYS SO; BUT IF YOU DARE, I'LL TEAR THE LOLLY-POPS FROM YOUR MEDDLING HAND."

EXTREMES MEET.

THE Half-breeds of Manitoba were in rebellion under the leadership of Louis Riel, on account of their alleged rights having been ignored in the bargain with the Hudson Bay Company. They demanded compensation for the land assumed by the Dominion. The artist cites this as a parallel to the position assumed by Mr. Howe on behalf of Nova Scotia, when " better terms " were demanded, and secured.

GRINCHUCKLE, JANUARY 27th, 1870.

EXTREMES MEET.

JOE (FROM THE EAST).—"GO IT! BE A PATRIOT; AND YOU'LL SELL WELL,—LIKE ME."

LOUIS (IN THE WEST).—"YOU'RE AN UNPRINCIPLED OLD SCAMP; BUT IF I DON'T GET MY $5000 A YEAR, BLOW ME TIGHT."

THE YOUNG LADY'S APPEAL TO A "GALLANT KNIGHT."

Sir Francis Hincks was the author of the Canadian "Shinplaster" currency, a scheme adopted to drive out the American silver. The cartoon will be understood from the following legend which accompanied it :—

Miss Canada : O, Sir Francis, I am suffering so much from this light American silver skate. It is no mate for the heavy gold one on my other foot. The doctors differ, but I shall never get along without another gold one.

Sir Francis H——s : The doctors be fiddled ! Who asked the doctors ? I'm your doctor ! You shall have the gold skate, my dear. Mr. Weir will attend to it. Meantime you can strengthen your ankle with a twenty-five cent Dominion plaster.

Miss Canada : A thousand thanks. Oh, I'm so glad ! (Aside : *But I'll burn the Plaster !*)

Sir Francis H——s (whose hearing is sharp) : I hope you will ?

Grinchuckle, February 10th, 1870.

THE YOUNG LADY'S APPEAL TO A "GALLANT KNIGHT."

THE MID-DAY GUN AT OTTAWA.

THIS cartoon is chiefly interesting as giving amusing portraits of a number of prominent parliamentarians. It is the custom to fire a gun from Nepean Point, opposite the House of Parliament, at twelve o'clock, noon, each day, which gives distinguished personages and others an opportunity of regulating their watches. At the date of this cartoon, workmen were engaged in making some additions to the central block.

CANADIAN ILLUSTRATED NEWS, MAY 11th, 1872.

THE MID-DAY GUN AT OTTAWA.

JOHN CANUCK'S NEW ROAD.

———————

GREAT dissatisfaction was expressed in the Maritime Provinces at the rejection of the St. John Valley route for the Intercolonial Railway. The change to the route subsequently selected—a much longer and costlier one— was made as the result of a conference with the Imperial authorities by Sir F. Hincks and Hon. Mr. Chandler, of New Brunswick. The contemplated expense of the road was a matter of serious concern, however, to all the Provinces.

CANADIAN ILLUSTRATED NEWS, MAY 11th, 1872.

JOHN CANUCK'S NEW ROAD.

Mr. John K. Nucke (a *gentleman farmer*).—" A fine balance at my banker's, eh! Glad to hear it! What's the next improvement you intend carrying out ?   For I've noticed a surplus always indicates some grand scheme concocted between you and the hands on the farm.   Now tell me; out with it ! "

Steward.—" Well, Your Honour ought to have a road made to the lake ; it would open up your property, and keep the hands busy, and——"

Mr. J. K. N.—" Well, well ! and what will it cost ? "

Steward.—" Oh ! a mere trifle ; some thirty millions or so ; and if that don't pay the contractor we will give him some of our waste land, you know.   We might spare 40 or 50 million acres and never feel it ! "

Mr. J. K. N.—" Whew ! (*whistle*).   Hem ! Ho, ho ! Well, we'll talk over it."

SCENE FROM THE MERRY WIVES OF WINDSOR.

An allusion to the annexation utterances of Hon. Joseph Howe. The figures in the group are Sir George E. Cartier, Sir John Macdonald, Sir Francis Hincks, and Mr. H. L. Langevin.

CANADIAN ILLUSTRATED NEWS, MARCH 30th, 1872.

SCENE FROM "THE MERRY WIVES OF WINDSOR."

SHALLOW.—"I HAVE LIVED FOUR-SCORE YEARS AND UPWARDS; I NEVER HEARD A MAN OF HIS PLACE, GRAVITY, AND LEARNING, SO WIDE OF HIS OWN RESPECT."—ACT III., SCENE I.

THE GAME OF SEE-SAW.

THE Maritime Provinces exhibited much fickleness in the bestowal of their political favor. In the first general election after Confederation only one supporter of the Conservative ministry was returned. In the next election, this state of affairs was exactly reversed.

CANADIAN ILLUSTRATED NEWS, MAY 4th, 1872.

A GAME OF SEE-SAW.

[SKETCHES FROM THE CAPITAL.]

THE MANY-COUNSELLED ULYSSES.

THIS was one of a series of sketches by Mr. E. Jump, in which he cleverly dressed leading Canadian politicians in the costumes and characters of classic heroes. The aptness of the delineation in this case will be recognized by all.

CANADIAN ILLUSTRATED NEWS, APRIL 12th, 1873.

THE MANY-COUNSELLED ULYSSES.

"Ulysses, first in public cares, she found,
For prudent counsels like the gods renowned."
[POPE, *Iliad II.*, 205, 6.]

AFTER THE SESSION."

On the 2nd of April, 1873, Honorable L. S. Huntington, member for
Shefford, from his place in the House, charged Sir John A. Macdonald with
having corruptly sold to Sir Hugh Allan the charter of the proposed
Canadian Pacific Railway, for a large sum of money, which had been used as
a Ministerial Bribery Fund in the preceding General Election.   Shortly after
this, and before any decided enquiry had been made into the matter, Parliament was adjourned (on May 23rd) until the following 13th of August.
The cartoon playfully suggests the feeling of the Opposition, represented by
Hon. A. Mackenzie, towards the accused Ministry during the " vacation."

Grip, May 31st, 1873.

"AFTER THE SESSION; OR, 'THE SITUATION.'"

J. A. M—C—D—N—LD.—"COME ON, OLD FELLOW, IT'S ALL RIGHT, YOU KNOW; IT'S MY TURN TO TREAT!"

A. M—K—NZ—E.—"OH, AYE, JONEY! BUT Y'MAUN RECOLLEC' I'M TE-TOTAL—MORE ESPEECIALLY TILL AUGUST!"

"CANADA'S LAOCOON."

AN adaptation of the classical story of Laocoon and the serpents to the circumstances of some of the parties to what was already known as the "Pacific Scandal." The persons represented are Sir Hugh Allan, (to whom the charter was sold), Sir John Macdonald, and Sir Francis Hincks. It is due to the latter gentleman to point out that, as indicated in the cartoon, he was merely *suspected* of complicity in the matter, and most emphatically denied the truth of the allegation of his guilt, made in some of the newspapers.

GRIP, JULY 19th, 1873.

"CANADA'S LAOCOON;"

OR, VIRGIL ON THE POLITICAL SITUATION.

"Ecce autem gemini a Tenedo, tranquilla per alta, &c."—Æneid, Book II.

(*Freely Translated.*)

"When lo ! two snakes (perhaps from the Yankee shore),
  Together trail their folds across the floor,
  With precious scandals reared in front they wind,

Charge after charge, in long drawn length behind !
While opposition benches cheer the while,
And John A. smiles a very ghastly smile !—and—"
              Everybody knows the rest !

" DUFFERIN'S TORMENTORS."

THE Ministerial party in the House, headed by Sir John Macdonald, were exceedingly anxious for a prorogation of Parliament,—the Opposition as earnestly opposed that course.   Their counter entreaties to the Governor-General on the subject suggested the familiar scene of the railway passenger and his friends the " cabbies."

GRIP, AUGUST 2nd, 1873.

"DUFFERIN'S TORMENTORS, OR *PER VIAS RECTAS*."

J—N A. (ANXIOUSLY).—"CARRIAGE, SIR? 'MINISTERIAL' HOTEL—ONLY CONSTITUTIONAL PLACE IN THE CITY—COME ALONG WITH ME, SIR."

Mc—K—NZ—(EAGERLY).—"THIS WAY, MY LORD—'REFORM' HOUSE! TAK' THE RIGHT COURSE—GIE' US YER CHECKS !!"

L—D D—FF—N.—"MUCH OBLIGED, GENTLEMEN, I ASSURE YOU; BUT I HAVE A 'RIG' OF MY OWN AT HAND, YOU KNOW."

"THE DAINTY DISH."

A NOTE here is perhaps superfluous. The faces of the "blackbirds" in the "pie" are those of Hon. M. Langevin, (a prominent member of the Macdonald Government), Sir Hugh Allan, James Beaty, Esq., (to represent the *Leader*), Sir John A. Macdonald, Sir Francis Hincks, "Uncle Sam," and T. C. Patteson, Esq., (representing the *Mail* newspaper). On Messrs. Blake and Mackenzie devolved the task of presenting the savory dish before Parliament.

GRIP, AUGUST 9th, 1873.

"ISN'T THAT A DAINTY DISH TO SET BEFORE A KING?"--Nursery Rhyme.

"WHITHER ARE WE DRIFTING."

GENERAL indignation was expressed throughout the country, when, in accordance with the advice of the implicated Premier, Parliament was prorogued, and the investigation of the scandal thus delayed. The words imputed to Sir John in the cartoon had been used by him on the floor of the House, and became a popular by-word while the discussion on the subject lasted.

GRIP, AUGUST 16th, 1873.

WHITHER ARE WE DRIFTING?

"THE BEAUTIES OF A ROYAL COMMISSION."

———————

THIS cartoon was intended to satirize the appointment by Sir John A. Macdonald of a Royal Commission, composed of his own friends, to inquire into and report upon the charges brought by the Hon. Mr. Huntington. The sentiment of the press and public with regard to this proceeding justified the implication of the caricature, that the accused Premier was virtually "trying himself."

GRIP, AUGUST 23rd, 1873.

THE BEAUTIES OF A ROYAL COMMISSION.

"WHEN SHALL WE THREE MEET AGAIN?"

"WAITING FOR HUNTINGTON."

———————

HON. MR. HUNTINGTON refused to acknowledge the Royal Commission appointed by the accused Minister, and declined to submit his case before it. The motive imputed to him by the Conservative press for this refusal was fear, and in·the eyes of his friends Sir John sustained the attitude represented in the cartoon.

GRIP, AUGUST 30th, 1873.

WAITING FOR HUNTINGTON!

"THE IRREPRESSIBLE SHOWMAN."

———————

APROPOS of the visit to Canada of Barnum, the Showman, during the Pacific Scandal "rever."

GRIP, SEPTEMBER 13, 1873.

THE IRREPRESSIBLE SHOWMAN.

BARNUM WANTS TO BUY THE "PACIFIC SCANDAL."

"BLACKWASH AND WHITEWASH."

―――――

"ILLUSTRATING," as the legend goes on to say, "the recent great Opposition speeches, and the doings of the jolly Royal Commission." The Reformers, of course, lost no opportunity of painting Sir John in grimy colors ; while it was generally acknowledged that the Royal Commissioners and the Conservative press did little more during the excitement than "whitewash" him.

GRIP, SEPTEMBER 20th, 1873.

BLACKWASH AND WHITEWASH.

ILLUSTRATING THE RECENT GREAT OPPOSITION SPEECHES, AND THE DOINGS OF THE JOLLY ROYAL COMMISSION.

"WE IN CANADA SEEM TO HAVE LOST ALL IDEA OF
JUSTICE, HONOR AND INTEGRITY."

So said the *Mail*, the leading Conservative organ, on September 26th. GRIP
sought to point this lugubrious confession with an illustration drawn from the
topic of the hour.

GRIP, SEPTEMBER 27th, 1873.

"WE IN CANADA SEEM TO HAVE LOST ALL IDEA OF JUSTICE, HONOR AND INTEGRITY."—The Mail, 26th September.

"PROGRESSING FAVORABLY."

A PEEP into the hearts of the Reform leaders during the interesting period of Sir John Macdonald's political "indisposition." The "Poor dear Premier" may be seen, if the reader will take the trouble to peer into the bedroom.

GRIP, OCTOBER 4th, 1873.

"PROGRESSING FAVORABLY."

MISS CANADA (ANXIOUSLY).—"DOCTORS, HOW DO YOU FIND THE POOR DEAR PREMIER?"

DR. B—N (FOR THE M.D.'S).—"MADAM, WE'VE JUST HAD A CONSULTATION; THE SYMPTOMS ARE HOPEFUL—WE BELIEVE HE CAN'T SURVIVE OCTOBER!"

"WILL HE GET THROUGH?"

THE question which was on all lips during the interim between the prorogation of the House of Commons on the 13th of August and the day fixed for
its re-assembling, October 23rd.   The prophecy conveyed in the unreason-
able smallness of the hoop in the clown's hand was duly realized.

GRIP, OCTOBER 18th, 1873.

"WILL HE GET THROUGH?"

"A CASE OF RIEL DISTRESS."

———

THE murder of Thomas Scott, at Fort Garry, during the Red River Rebellion, naturally excited great indignation throughout the Dominion, and a universal demand was made for the apprehension and punishment of Louis Riel, the leader of the malcontents, at whose instigation the deed was committed. This righteous sentiment, however, ultimately resolved itself into mere political "claptrap," the Conservative Government, then in power, having secretly promised the rebels an amnesty, while publicly professing an anxious desire to "catch him."

GRIP, OCTOBER 25th, 1873.

A CASE OF <u>RIEL</u> DISTRESS!

"THE IRREPRESSIBLE JACK."

THE circumstances under which Sir John Macdonald was deposed from power seemed to warrant the assumption of the Reformers that he was "done for." But, on the contrary, it only seemed the signal for additional honors to be heaped upon him by the Conservative Party, who unhesitatingly chose him leader of the Opposition, and nominated him as member for Kingston, West Toronto, etc., not to mention banquets, and other species of emphasis.

GRIP, NOVEMBER 22nd, 1873.

THE IRREPRESSIBLE JACK; OR, THE CONSERVATIVE RESUSCITATION.

JOHN A. (SIDE SHOWMAN)—"DID YOU THINK THE LITTLE FELLER'S SPRING WAS BROKE, MY DEARS?"

"THE PREMIER'S MODEL."

In an address to the electors of Lambton, soon after the accession to power of the Reform Party, Mr. Mackenzie declared the cardinal points of the Policy he would inaugurate, as leader, to be "Electoral Purity" and "the Independence of Parliament." (Before entering political life, Mr. Mackenzie followed the vocation of stone-mason.)

Grip, November 29th, 1873.

THE PREMIER'S MODEL;

OR, "IMPLEMENTS TO THOSE WHO CAN USE THEM."

CANADA—"WELL AND BRAVELY DONE, MACKENZIE; NOW STAND BY THAT POLICY, AND I'M WITH YOU ALWAYS!"

"THE POLITICAL GIANT-KILLER."

THE " Canada First " movement, having for its object the cultivation of a national sentiment and the extinction of political party strife, was inaugurated about this time.

GRIP, DECEMBER 13th, 1873.

THE POLITICAL GIANT-KILLER; OR, "CANADA FIRST."

"CHRISTMAS PIE."

The treat which Santa Claus had in store for the Reformers.

Grip, December 27th, 1873.

"CHRISTMAS PIE."

"THE CRUEL OBJECT OF DISSOLUTION."

Mr. Mackenzie and his colleagues advised the dissolution of Parliament on taking office. This was accordingly carried out, with the object, as the cartoon suggests, of keeping Sir John and his comrades " out in the cold."

Grip, January 10th, 1874.

THE CRUEL OBJECT OF "DISSOLUTION."

"PITY THE DOMINIE; OR, JOHNNY'S RETURN."

ANENT the re-election of Sir John A. Macdonald as member for Kingston, in the general election which followed the accession of the Reform Government.

GRIP, FEBRUARY 7th, 1874.

PITY THE DOMINIE; OR, JOHNNY'S RETURN.

CANADA—"HERE'S OUR JOHNNY FOR YOU AGAIN, MR. MACKENZIE! YOU'LL FIND HIM APT ENOUGH, BUT FRANKLY, SIR, HE'S FULL OF MISCHIEF!"

"THE NEW DEPARTURE."

Hon. Edward Blake's withdrawal from the new Government, very shortly after it had taken possession of the Treasury Benches, created an unpleasant sensation throughout the country. The hon. gentleman had been perhaps the main instrument in bringing about a fall of the preceding Cabinet.

Grip, February 21st, 1874.

THE NEW DEPARTURE.

Spouse B——e.—"FAREWELL FOR THE PRESENT, DEAR; YOU AND THE GIRLS MUST MANAGE THE HOUSE IN MY ABSENCE!"

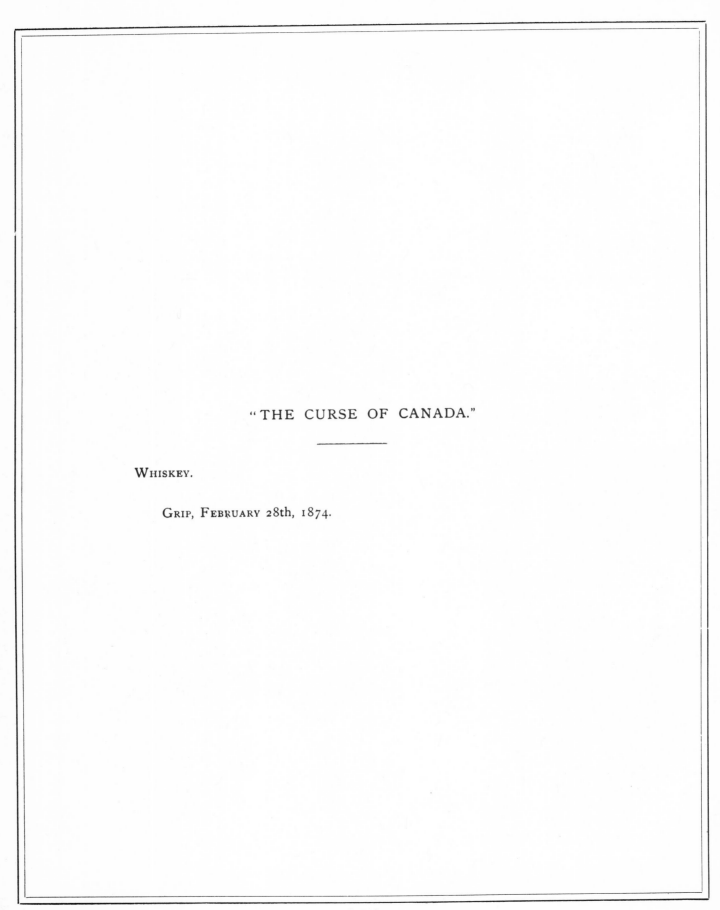

"THE CURSE OF CANADA."

WHISKEY.

GRIP, FEBRUARY 28th, 1874.

THE CURSE OF CANADA.

IS THERE NO ARM TO SAVE?

"'GRIP'S' PERPETUAL COMEDY."

THE adjournment of the Ontario Legislature was immediately followed by the assembling of the Dominion Parliament at Ottawa.

GRIP, MARCH 28th, 1874.

"GRIP'S" PERPETUAL COMEDY.

"THEY HAVE THEIR EXITS AND THEIR ENTRANCES."

"THE VACANT CHAIR."

Louis Riel, the leader of the Red River Rebellion and alleged murderer of Thomas Scott, had been returned for Provencher, Manitoba, to the Dominion Parliament. He prudently failed to take his seat in the House, while the unanimity with which both sides cried for his arrest made "the vacant chair" a bond of union for the time being.

Grip, April 4th, 1874.

THE VACANT CHAIR.

A *RIEL* BOND OF UNION.

"THE SCIENCE OF CHEEK."

A GREAT sensation was caused throughout the country at the announcement that Riel had actually appeared in the House at Ottawa and signed the Members' Roll. This he did *incog.*, and immediately afterwards disappeared. The cartoon anticipated his next step in the " Science of Cheek."

GRIP, APRIL 11th, 1874.

THE SCIENCE OF CHEEK; OR, RIEL'S NEXT MOVE.

RIEL (LOQ.)—"FIVE TOUSSAND DOLLARS! BY GAR, I SHALL ARREST ZE SCOUNDREL MYSELF!"

"A TOUCHING APPEAL."

On the accession of Mr. Mackenzie's Government a large deficit in the treasury was discovered. Mr. (now Sir Richard) Cartwright, Finance Minister, in his Budget speech, attributed this to the extravagance and corruption of the preceding Administration. A new tariff was issued, in which the duties on various articles were raised considerably.

Grip, April 18th, 1874.

A TOUCHING APPEAL.

("TOUCHING" THE SECRET OF INCREASED TAXATION.)

YOUNG CANADA "SAY, UNCLE JOHN, WON'T YOU GIVE ME A 'DEFICIT?' MA SAYS YOU GAVE THE GRITS ONE!"

"MRS. GAMP'S HOME-THRUST."

EARLY in the session a committee was appointed to inquire into the cause of the North-West difficulties, and during the progress of the inquiry evidence was elicited (mainly from Archbishop Tache) which implicated Sir John A. Macdonald. The Reform Party is represented in the cartoon as facetiously anticipating a repetition of the right hon. gentleman's famous asseveration of his innocence.

GRIP, MAY 2nd, 1874.

MRS. GAMP'S HOME-THRUST.

SAIREY GAMP (THE REFORM PARTY)—"'AVEN'T GOT NOTHINK TO SAY ABOUT THEM 'ANDS THIS TIME, I SUPPOGE, MISTER SIR JOHN?'

"PACIFIC PASTIMES."

THE Reform Government took up the Pacific Railway scheme, but initiated a new policy with regard to it. Sir John Macdonald had pledged the country to complete the entire work within ten years. Mr. Mackenzie characterized this as a physical impossibility, and proposed, as the cartoon has it, " to tak' the distance in sensible like jumps, ye ken!"

GRIP, MAY 16th, 1874.

PACIFIC PASTIMES; OR, THE HARD "ROAD TO TRAVEL."

"DIGNITY" WITHOUT "IMPUDENCE."

THE Dominion Senate, usually so passive and quiet, strikingly signalized its life and vim during this session by throwing out a bill introduced by Mr. Cameron, M.P. for South Huron, having for its object the re-distribution of the electoral divisions composing that Riding.

GRIP, MAY 23rd, 1874.

"DIGNITY" WITHOUT "IMPUDENCE."

OLD MADAME SENATE—"I SAY, MR. LOWER-HOUSE MACKENZIE, WHO'S RUNNING THIS COUNTRY, ANYHOW?"

JUSTICE AND GENEROSITY.

Hon. (now Sir) A. A. Dorion, a prominent leader of the Rouge or French Reform Party, occupied the office of Minister of Justice in the Government of Hon. Alexander Mackenzie. In this capacity he offered to himself in the capacity of an able lawyer, a seat upon the Bench of his Province, which offer was gratefully accepted. He still occupies the position (1886).

Grip, July 6th, 1874.

JUSTICE & GENEROSITY; OR, "HOIST WITH HIS OWN"—PREROGATIVE.

MRS. MINISTER OF JUSTICE DORION (TO THE HON. A. A. DITTO)—"HE WAS A GOOD 'ITTLE GRITTSY-TITTSY, SO HE WAS,
AND HE SHALL HAVE A NICE 'ITTLE SOFT SEATSY-TEETSY, SO HE SHALL!"

ST. GEORGE AND THE DRAGON.

As an outcome of reckless malice, amidst the passionate decisions of politics about this time, one of the Conservative papers published a scandalous libel reflecting upon the Hon. George Brown's private character.   With characteristic promptitude the assailed gentleman had the paper indicted, and a full apology was made.   To those who knew Mr. Brown, there was no need of his trouble in this matter, but the event served as an illustration of his uncompromising self-respect.

GRIP, AUGUST 8th, 1874.

"SAINT GEORGE AND THE DRAGON."

THE PLAIN FACT.

THE amended election law (introduced by the government of Mr. Mackenzie) was purposely made very stringent as a measure against bribery and corruption, and at this time trials were first conducted under its provisions. It so happened that the first victims were members of the party that had passed the measure, but the slaughter was by no means confined to that party. The expression " Come along, John, and put down bribery and corruption " had been imputed to a supporter of one of the unseated members, in the course of the election trial of Col. Walker, the member elect, at London, and for a considerable time the phrase was one of the catch-words of the Conservative Party. ·

GRIP, SEPTEMBER 19th, 1874.

THE PLAIN FACT.

MACKENZIE—"COME ALONG, JOHN, AND PUT DOWN BRIBERY AND CORRUPTION; NEITHER OF US CAN RIDE YON
MULE YET AWHILE."

SIX AND HALF A DOZEN.

As a reply to the jibes of the *Globe* on the subject of political corruption, the Conservative party recalled the record of Mr. George Brown in the Brown *vs.* Gibbs contest in South Ontario, some years previously. This election, it was alleged, had been characterized by glaring instances of bribery on the Reform side ; but there was, in those days, little or no legal restraint put upon such tactics.

GRIP, NOVEMBER 28th, 1874.

SIX AND HALF A DOZEN.

SIR JOHN—"MR. BROWN, DO YOU THINK YOU COULD GO THROUGH THIS HOOP AS WELL AS I WENT THROUGH THAT ONE, IF YOU HAD A "TRIAL"?

CHRISTMAS MORNING.

In accordance with the time-honored custom Mr. Grip fills the stockings of his *proteges* with good things, in recognition of Christmas, which comes " but once a year."

Grip, December 26th, 1874.

CHRISTMAS MORNING; OR, THE POLITICAL STOCKINGS.

LOYALTY IN A QUANDARY.

In the House of Commons, Sir John Macdonald sought to make a point against the Mackenzie Government for having declared an amnesty to those concerned in the Half-breed rebellion in Manitoba, which amnesty included Lepine, one of the rebel leaders, who had been condemned to death. As, at this time, the prerogative of clemency was vested in the Crown, the action to which exception was taken was that of the Governor-General and not of the Government. By the efforts of Hon. Edward Blake, a change was subsequently made in the Governor-General's instructions, by which the responsibility in this, as in other matters, was vested in the Government.

GRIP, FEBRUARY 6th, 1875.

LOYALTY IN A QUANDARY; OR, THE "LEPINE CASE" MADE PLAIN.

OTHELLO BROWN'S APOLOGY.

HON. GEORGE BROWN had undertaken a mission to Washington, on behalf of the Government, to secure a reciprocity treaty between the United States and Canada, but was unsuccessful in his efforts. Mr. Brown was now a prominent member of the Canadian Senate.

GRIP, FEBRUARY 27th, 1875.

OTHELLO BROWN'S APOLOGY,

BEFORE THE SENATE, FEBRUARY 15th, 1875.

WAITING FOR THE SIGNAL.

THE growing sentiment of the country against the liquor traffic had been voiced in Parliament by Mr. G. W. Ross, a member of the Reform Party. The Government expressed a willingness to consider the subject of Legal Prohibition as soon as they had evidence that a majority of the people desired such a measure. Rev. Mr. Afflick, an eloquent English lecturer, was at this time making a tour of Canada in the interest of the temperance cause.

GRIP, MARCH 6th, 1875.

WAITING FOR THE SIGNAL.

THE POLITICAL SPELLING-SCHOOL.

THE popular craze at this date was "Spelling Matches." The persons represented in the cartoon were prominent members of the respective parties ; those on the left (Conservative) being : Sir John A. Macdonald, Hon. M. C. Cameron, Messrs. P. Mitchell, Beatty, Patteson, Bunster, Alonzo Wright and Rykert ; on the right (Reform) Messrs. Brown, Blake, Mackenzie, Laird, McKellar and Mowat, with Mr. Goldwin Smith. Mr. Samuel Platt, M.P., for East Toronto, had just passed successfully through the ordeal of an election trial, and is commended for his correct spelling of " Purity," a word which had often bothered some of the other boys.

GRIP, MAY 1st, 1875.

GRIP'S POLITICAL SPELLING MATCH.

PERFECT FREEDOM! O, FOR LIBERTY!

MR. MACKENZIE was at this time on a visit to his native country, where he was honored with the freedom of Perth and Dundee, and otherwise handsomely recognized.   It had long been a common saying in Canada that Mr. George Brown, through the *Globe*, exercised a supreme influence over the Reform Government.

GRIP, JULY 24th, 1875

PERFECT FREEDOM! O, FOR LIBERTY!

THE POLITICAL SITUATION.

Mr. Goldwin Smith's teachings on the subject of " No Partyism " excited
the hostility of both Grit and Tory partizans, and his position between the
Globe and *Mail* was precisely that of the hapless school-boy pictured in the
chromo of which the cartoon is an adaptation.

Grip, July 31st, 1875.

THE POLITICAL SITUATION.

(ADAPTED FROM A POPULAR CHROMO.)

INCONSISTENT PRACTICE OF FREE TRADE DR. BROWN.

Mr. George Brown was an earnest advocate of the Free Trade principle in political economy, and was always vigorous in his denunciation of the opposite principle in any direction. About this time the *Globe* had earnestly denounced the action of the Ontario Society of Physicians and Surgeons for having prosecuted an unlicensed practitioner, under a law which the *Globe* always regarded as narrow and tyrannical. This was not very consistent with the attitude it sustained towards Mr. Goldwin Smith as a healer of the body politic. Mr. Alderman Baxter, well-known in Toronto, is used as a metaphorical figure of Justice.

Grip, September 4th, 1875.

INCONSISTENT "PRACTICE" OF FREE TRADE DR. BROWN.

PISTOLS FOR THREE.

Rev. Egerton Ryerson, D.D., was drawn into the Brown-Smith controversy, and it soon became what is known as a "game of cut-throat"—each against the others. Grip, believing that, in the stereotyped newspaper phrase, "this correspondence had gone on long enough," was tempted to suggest a fatal shot all round as perhaps the only way of securing a "rest" for the reading public.

Grip, September 11th, 1875.

PISTOLS FOR THREE; OR, THE TRIANGULAR "DUEL."

CANADIAN POLITICS: A PICTURE FOR THE PARTIES.

Mr. Goldwin Smith continued his attacks upon Partyism with unabated vigor in the columns of the *Nation* and the *Canadian Monthly*, his contention being that the chief end and aim of both " factions " was office.

Grip, September 25th, 1875.

CANADIAN POLITICS: A PICTURE FOR THE "PARTIES."

POLITICAL PURITY; OR, POT AND KETTLE.

Mr. George Brown had written a letter to a political friend—Senator Simpson—asking for a contribution towards the election fund of the Reform Party in the heat of the general election. This letter was secured by the Conservative Party, and commented upon as a set-off to the celebrated telegram of Sir John Macdonald, calling upon Sir Hugh Allan for " another $10,000." Mr. Brown vigorously denied that he had used any of the money contributed for other than legitimate expenses, or that his letter had been written with any corrupt intent.

Grip, October 2nd, 1875.

POLITICAL PURITY; OR, POT AND KETTLE.

THE MINISTERIAL SHANTY.

MR. JOSEPH CAUCHON, a prominent representative of Quebec, was taken into the Mackenzie Cabinet. M. Cauchon had, some time previously, been denounced by Mr. Brown, in connection with an episode in his Provincial career, as a most unworthy man. The incident referred to—that of making a speculation at the expense of the inmates of the Beauport Asylum at Quebec—was characterized by Mr. Brown as an offence that was "rank and smelled to heaven," and this expression was constantly quoted by the Tory press during M. Cauchon's connection with the Ministry.

GRIP, DECEMBER 18th, 1875.

THE MINISTERIAL SHANTY; OR, THE CAUCHON AT HOME.

THE PRINCE OF ORANGE.

Hon. Mackenzie Bowell occupied a high place in the Conservative ranks by virtue of his connection with the Orange Order ; Sir Hector Langevin was regarded as similarly representing Ultramontane views. Politically and personally they were warm friends and colleagues. The cartoon was a satirical allusion to some Orange " bounce " that had been indulged in by Mr. Bowell out of the House.

Grip, February 19th, 1876.

THE "PRINCE OF ORANGE;" OR, ANYTHING TO BEAT THE GOVERNMENT.

RUNNING BEFORE THE PROTECTION WIND.

———————

THE Conservative Party, becoming weary of the cold shades of opposition, took advantage of the "hard times" to proclaim a policy of Protection to Home Industries as the only salvation for the country. The Government, it was alleged, was largely responsible for the depression, and could relieve it only by raising the tariff. This cry seemed to meet with popular approval.

GRIP, MARCH 18th, 1876.

RUNNING BEFORE THE PROTECTION WIND.

EATING THE LEEK; OR, "HENRY V." AS LATELY PLAYED IN THE COMMONS.

Mr. Mackenzie had been charged with nepotism in connection with the purchase of steel rails for the C. P. R.—the contract for the purchase having been awarded to a firm in which it was alleged the Premier's brother had an interest. This charge had been repeated frequently upon the hustings, although Mr. Mackenzie had demonstrated that it was unfounded. His explanation upon the floor of Parliament at this time gave the final death blow to the slander.

Grip, April 8th, 1876.

EATING THE LEEK;

OR, "HENRY V." AS LATELY PLAYED IN THE COMMONS.

FLUELLAN.—MR. MACKENZIE.   PISTOL.—DR. TUPPER.

THE DEPRESSION COMMITTEE SIMPLIFIED.

———————

THE Protection agitation induced the Government to appoint a committee to investigate the causes of the Depression of Trade. This committee was composed mainly of Government supporters, well known to be free-traders, and its report was to the effect that a Protective Tariff would not cure the difficulty, which arose from causes beyond Governmental control.

GRIP, APRIL 29th, 1876.

THE "DEPRESSION COMMITTEE" SIMPLIFIED.

OFF WITH HIS HEAD.

THE Crooks Act, a measure intended to further restrict the evils of the liquor traffic, came into force at this time.   Under the provisions of this Act the number of licenses to be issued by any municipality was limited, and the consequence was a wholesale " decapitation " of liquor sellers throughout the Province.   The Act was framed by Hon. Adam Crooks, and in the cartoon is being appropriately carried out by Hon. O. Mowat, the head of the " Executive."

GRIP, MAY 6th, 1876.

OFF WITH HIS HEAD!

"RICHARD III.," AS PLAYED BY MR. CROOKS THROUGHOUT THE PROVINCE.

TRYING TO SMUGGLE ACROSS.

———

SIR JOHN MACDONALD had so far recovered his self-assurance by this time, that he and his followers were calmly asserting that there really was " nothing in " the Pacific Scandal. The Conservative press had in fact ceased to call it a " Scandal " at all ; " Slander " was the word now used. The possibility that Sir John could so far regain the confidence of the Canadian people as to get back to office was amongst the things the *Globe* regarded as ridiculous.

GRIP, JULY 29th, 1876.

TRYING TO SMUGGLE ACROSS.

POLICEMAN G. B.—"NOTHING IN IT! THEN WHY NOT VINDICATE YOURSELF BY HAVING IT THOROUGHLY EXAMINED."

THE ONLY SATISFYING PICNIC AFTER ALL.

WHILE the Reformers were enjoying the good things of office, Sir John and his principal colleagues were passing the summer in making a picnic tour. The political picnic had become of late years a Canadian institution, and although there were pleasures to be derived from the outings in the leafy woods, with their accompanying buns, lemonade and political addresses, these were not to be compared to the attractions of the Treasury Benches.

GRIP, AUGUST 19th, 1876.

THE ONLY SATISFYING PICNIC, AFTER ALL!

BRANDED.

THE *Mail* proved a most vigorous and alert Oppositionist and lost no opportunity for an attack upon the Government, whether fair or foul. For the sake of political capital it did not hesitate to " run down " the country, and thus to furnish the European press with arguments against emigration to Canada. The incident which called forth the cartoon was the *Mail's* endorsation of a baseless slander on Canada which had been forwarded to the London *Times* from California.

GRIP, SEPTEMBER 2nd, 1876.

BRANDED!

FOR ENDORSING UNFOUNDED SLANDERS AGAINST CANADA.

CONFEDERATION, THE MUCH-FATHERED YOUNGSTER.

———

ALTHOUGH the historical facts as to the origin of the idea of Confederation were familiar to most intelligent Canadians, (and they by no means the oldest inhabitants,) there was a standing dispute as to the party to whom the honor of its paternity belonged. Claims were put forth (amongst others,) on behalf of Messrs. George Brown, Sir F. Hincks, Wm. Macdougall and Sir John A. Macdonald.

GRIP, SEPTEMBER 30th, 1876.

CONFEDERATION!

THE MUCH-FATHERED YOUNGSTER.

THE TRANSPARENT FACTS.

His Excellency the Governor-General (Lord Dufferin) undertook a mission to British Columbia, in connection with a vice-regal visit, to bring about, if possible, a good understanding between that Province and the Dominion on the subject of the projected Canada Pacific Railway. The British Columbians were at the moment in a state of great excitement over what they regarded as a breach of faith by the Federal Government, and were even threatening secession. Lord Dufferin was, as usual, successful in his efforts at peace-making. The " transparent facts " given in the cartoon detail the various stages of the difficulty up to the date of Lord Dufferin's intervention.

Grip, October 7th, 1876.

THE TRANSPARENT FACTS.

IN THE MATTER OF THE "CARNARVON TERMS."

THE CONSERVATIVE POSITION.

THAT the adoption of the Protective Policy was a mere piece of political tactics on the part of the Conservative leader was demonstrated in every move from first to last. He and his chief supporters in Parliament had been throughout their whole public career adherents of the revenue-tariff system equally with their opponents, and it was asking too much of public credulity to require the people to believe that they had been soundly converted to Protectionism in a moment, and that moment just before a general election when there was wide-spread grumbling at the hard times.

GRIP, DECEMBER 2nd, 1876.

THE CONSERVATIVE POSITION.

PADDY MACDONALD.—"BEGORRA, I DON'T CARE FWITCH IT'LL TAKE ME TO, AV IT ONLY TAKES ME TO ME OWLD PLACE AT OTTAWAY."

NOT A REAL LION.

———————

AT the numerous political picnics throughout the country, Sir John and his lieutenants were loud in their denunciations of the Government in connection with various scandals. In the presence of their opponents in Parliament, however, they refrained from formulating their charges or pressing for investigation.

GRIP, FEBRUARY 17th, 1877.

NOT A REAL LION—EXCEPT OUTSIDE THE HOUSE.

JOHN A.—"You ladies, you, whose gentle hearts do fear .
When lion rough in wildest rage doth roar, (at picnics, etc.)
Then know that I, one 'John the Trickster,' am
A lion's fell nor else no lion's dam."—*Midsummer Night's Dream.*

WHAT INVESTIGATION REVEALED.

DURING the Session of Parliament some startling facts were made known as to the relations of the Northern Railway Company to the late Government. The Company was deeply indebted to the Dominion, and had been making vigorous efforts to get the amount reduced. For the purpose of influencing favorable legislation to this end, it was found that large sums of money had been contributed to the Conservative funds in various elections, and also that money had been subscribed on behalf of the Company to a cash testimonial presented to Sir John himself, and for stock in the *Mail* newspaper. The transaction was vigorously denounced by the Reform and Independent press as a specimen of brazen corruption.

GRIP, APRIL 7th, 1877.

WHAT INVESTIGATION REVEALED.

WHAT THE CHIEFTAIN HEARD.

———

SIR JOHN professed to hear a universal demand for the reinstatement of himself and colleagues in office. It was not doubted that some sound had reached his ears, but GRIP's view was that this sound was but the echo of his own anxious voice. In this GRIP was mistaken, however.

GRIP, JULY 14th, 1877.

WHAT THE CHIEFTAIN HEARD.

"WHEN I WAS IN THE EASTERN TOWNSHIPS, I HEARD THE CRY ECHOING FROM ROCK TO ROCK, ACROSS THE BOSOMS OF THOSE BEAUTIFUL LAKES, AND OVER THE EMERALD FIELD,—'COME TO OUR RESCUE, JOHN A., OR WE ARE LOST.'"

[SIR JOHN'S SPEECH AT MONTREAL. SEE THE MAIL, JULY 9TH.]

LET US HAVE PEACE.

THE *Globe* exerted all its influence to allay the bad feeling which had been manifested in connection with the Montreal riots between Orangemen and Catholics, and which existed in many other parts of the country. It was strongly opposed, however, to the policy of prohibiting party processions by law, as this only tended to intensify the evil.

GRIP, AUGUST 4th, 1877.

LET US HAVE PEACE;

OR, THE BEST WAY TO END THE "PROCESSION" DIFFICULTY.

TEACHING THE POLLY-TICIANS WHAT TO SAY.

THE Pacific Scandal was by this date so far "Ancient History" that the facts of the case had undergone a complete metamorphosis as given out by the Tory orators. It was now the fashionable thing in that party to repeat the watchword given in the cartoon.

GRIP, SEPTEMBER 8th, 1877.

TEACHING THE POLLY-TICIANS WHAT TO SAY.

HIS BEST FRIEND DESERTING HIM.

———————

THE main hope of the Opposition in view of the general election was in the capital that was being made out of the depression of trade. A slight improvement was noticeable in the business outlook at the date of this cartoon.

GRIP, OCTOBER 20th, 1877.

HIS BEST FRIEND DESERTING HIM.

SCARING THE MARITIME HORSE.

THE free-trade sentiment in the Maritime Provinces was known to be strong, and it was thought that the advocacy of the National Policy would endanger the seats of the Conservatives in that section of the country. Sir Charles Tupper was the leading representative of his party from the Lower Provinces, and was one of the most efficient supporters of the Protection idea. The event proved, however, that Sir Charles understood the temper of the people down by the sea better than the theorists, as the N. P. was handsomely sustained in that part of the country.

GRIP, NOVEMBER 24th, 1877.

SCARING THE MARITIME HORSE.

SETTLING THE ACCOUNT.

THE arbitrators appointed to decide the dispute between Canada and the United States in reference to the Fisheries had awarded the sum of $5,500,000 to the Dominion as compensation for damages sustained at the hands of American fishermen. To this award Mr. Kellogg, the American representative, had dissented, and had afterwards sought to invalidate the award on the ground that the decision had not been unanimous. The United States had not at that time—and have not yet—paid to England the large balance remaining fromt he Geneva award, promptly paid by the latter Power in connection with the " Alabama " claims.

GRIP, DECEMBER 1st, 1877.

SETTLING THE ACCOUNT.

JONATHAN.—"CRAWL OUT OF THAT LOOP-HOLE? HUNKERSLIDE? NEVER! KELLOGG, NEVER! I'LL PAY 'EM THE AWARD NOBLY—
WITH THEIR OWN MONEY!"

SITTING ON THE POOR MAN.

————————

An agitation for the abolition of the system of exemption from taxation had been started in the newspapers. The injustice of exempting various officials who enjoyed good salaries, and imposing a corresponding heavy burden upon those less able to bear it, was earnestly denounced, and the Ontario Government were called upon to introduce a measure to cure the evil. No action has, however, been taken up to the present time.

Grip, January 19th, 1878.

The sign reads:

NO
CLASS LEGISLATION
IN
THIS FREE COUNTRY!

DOWN WITH EXEMPTION

LET
EVERY MAN
PAY HIS FAIR SHARE
OF THE
TAXES!!

(SIGNED)
JOHN HALLAM.
(AND EVERY OTHER)
SENSIBLE MAN

SITTING ON THE POOR MAN; OR, THE INJUSTICE OF EXEMPTION.

ANCIENT TROY TACTICS.

THIS was still another repetition of the opinion that the Tory Party, in adopting the National Policy, had in view the one grand object of "getting in" to office. The allusion is of course to the familiar classic story of the method adopted by the Greeks to gain admission to Troy.

GRIP, JULY 6th, 1878.

ANCIENT TROY TACTICS
OR

THE TRULY LOYAL BOY ALARMING THE MASTER.

A GREAT outcry was made by the *Globe* on the alleged anti-British tendency of the National Policy as announced by the Conservative leaders during the campaign.   To the alarming statement that it would inevitably weaken British connection, the leading organ of the Opposition responded—" so much the worse for British connection.'

GRIP, JULY 27th, 1878.

THE TRULY LOYAL BOY ALARMING THE MASTER.

ALL AT SEA.

ANOTHER allusion to the ludicrous contradictions and inconsistencies of the principal advocates of the National Policy in their public speeches, when, in response to the popular demand, they undertook to "come down to particulars" as to what that Policy was to be

GRIP, AUGUST 17th, 1878

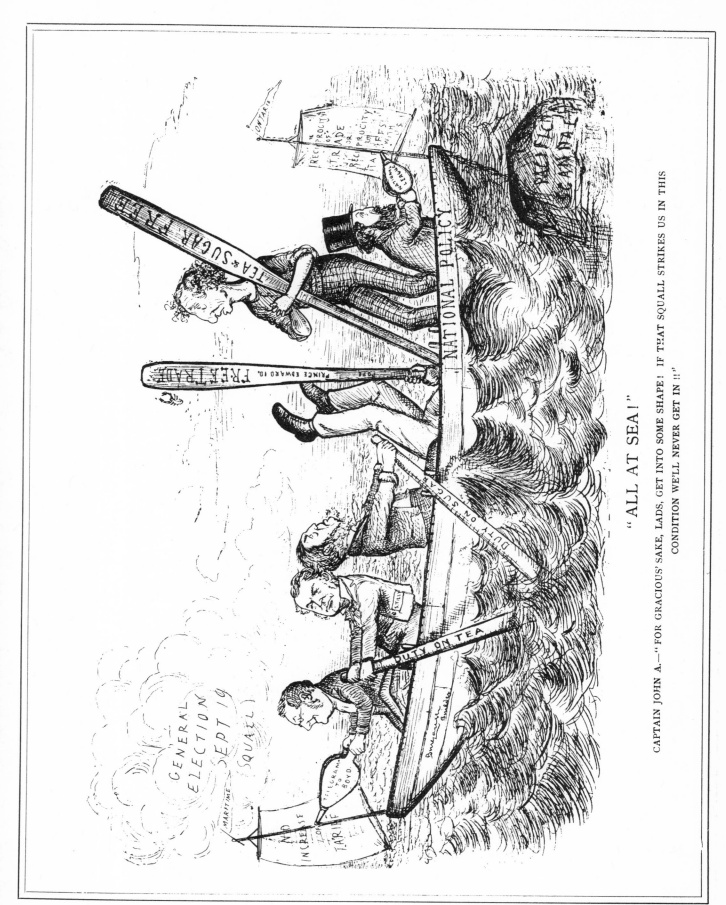

"ALL AT SEA!"

CAPTAIN JOHN A.—"FOR GRACIOUS' SAKE, LADS, GET INTO SOME SHAPE! IF THAT SQUALL STRIKES US IN THIS
CONDITION WE'LL NEVER GET IN !!"

RENEWING THE LEASE.

THIS bold prophecy was made on the assumption that the people of Canada clearly saw through the game of the newly-made Protectionists, and that the circumstances under which Sir John and his colleagues had demitted office in 1873 would preclude the possibility of their success on this occasion.

GRIP, SEPTEMBER 14th, 1878.

RENEWING THE LEASE.

MISS CANADA (TO JOHN A.)—"YOU WANT THE FARM AGAIN! YOU LEFT IT IN A SHOCKING CONDITION FIVE YEARS AGO, AND THE PRESENT TENANT HAS ALMOST RESTORED IT BY HIS INDUSTRY. YOUR 'PLAN' LOOKS BOGUS. I WILL RENEW MACKENZIE'S LEASE."

O, OUR PROPHETIC SOUL!

THE general election which came off on the 17th resulted in a sweeping victory for Sir John and the National Policy, and Mr. GRIP's artist humbly took his place amongst the false prophets.

GRIP, SEPTEMBER 21st, 1878.

O, OUR PROPHETIC SOUL!

(See last week's Cartoon.)

JOHN A.—"I DON'T KNOW, BUT IT SEEMS TO ME THIS PICTURE OF YOURS, MY PROPHETIC FRIEND, NEEDS A LITTLE 'RE-ADJUSTMENT,' DON'T IT, HEY?"

THE BEST OF FRIENDS MUST PART.

To the hard times Sir John and his Party were primarily indebted for their present good fortune, but (contrary to the hopes of the innocents who had implicitly accepted the anti-election promises of the N. P. advocates) prosperity did not immediately return. The persistency with which the depression continued to " hang on " was a source of much annoyance to the Government, as it was the constant theme of ridicule in the Reform press.

GRIP, NOVEMBER 2nd, 1878.

"THE BEST OF FRIENDS MUST PART!"

JOHN A.—"WELL, GOOD-BY, OLD FELLOW; THANKS VERY MUCH FOR YOUR HELP DURING THE CAMPAIGN; BUT DON'T LET ME DETAIN YOU NOW.   GOOD-BY, *AU REVOIR*, ADIEU, FAREWELL, TRA-LA-LA, TA-TA."

HARD TIMES.—"CERTINGLY; BUT I AIN'T GONE YET, ME HEARTY!"

THE COMING ATTRACTION.

THIS was an allusion to the opening of Parliament on February 13th prox., and the questions then to be brought forward. The principal matters anticipated were the introduction of the promised National Policy ; the settlement of the Letellier difficulty and the C. P. Railway.

GRIP, JANUARY 11th, 1879.

THE COMING ATTRACTION!

"HERE HE COMES!

PARLIAMENT was now in Session, and the introduction of the much talked of Tariff was momentarily expected. The Oppositionists were eager for the fray. The Cartoon is an adaptation of one of Woolf's *Gamin* sketches.

GRIP, FEBRUARY 15th, 1879

"HERE HE COMES!"

IN THE RING AT LAST.

―――――――

THE Budget Speech was delivered during the preceding week, and the principal contents of the new Tariff are displayed upon the "Elephant"—a symbol, by the way, which had been adopted to express GRIP's opinion that the National Policy would ultimately prove to be a source of embarrassment to its authors.

GRIP, MARCH 22nd, 1879.

IN THE RING AT LAST!

THE TALENTED ELEPHANT'S FIRST ACT.

GOODS PROHIBITED BUT *EVILS* ADMITTED.

WHILE the National Policy carefully excluded American goods of various kinds, it of course afforded no protection against the entry of American " Evils," and amongst these the Rag-money agitation ; anti-Chinese politics, etc., had already begun to take root in Canada.

GRIP, APRIL 26th, 1879.

GOODS PROHIBITED, BUT *EVILS* ADMITTED.

MISS CANADA.—"NOW, MR. PREMIER, I DON'T PROPOSE TO ALLOW THIS COUNTRY TO BE MADE A SLAUGHTER-MARKET FOR AMERICAN IDEAS, ANY MORE THAN FOR AMERICAN GOODS."

SIR JOHN'S CROWNING VICTORY.

DURING a visit to England at this time Sir John Macdonald was honored by being made a Privy Councillor.

GRIP, AUGUST 23rd, 1879.

SIR JOHN'S CROWNING VICTORY.

CLEAR THE TRACK.

THE popular feeling against the second chamber plan continued to grow, and received new impetus from time to time from the frivolous, dishonest or partizan conduct of the Dominion Senate. Those provinces which still retained Legislative Councils began to see in the success of Ontario with a single chamber that they were enduring an unnecessary expense. As to the Senate, the popular view was and is that it must either be abolished or made elective.

GRIP, SEPTEMBER 13th, 1879.

THEIR USEFULNESS BEING GONE, THESE SECOND CHAMBER OLD LADIES WILL HAVE TO

CLEAR THE TRACK!

A QUEER COINCIDENCE.

A NOTICEABLE improvement in the commercial outlook had recently set in, and was hailed by the Conservative Party as conclusive proof that prosperity and Conservative rule were synonymous terms. The Opposition were correspondingly depressed at the apparent countenance Providence had given to what they had always denounced as an absurdity.

GRIP, OCTOBER 4th, 1879.

THE "QUEER COINCIDENCE."

G. B.—"I WONDER WHY THIS UNSAVORY TRAMP DISNA FOLLOW YON OTHER PAIRTY, BUT ALWAYS CLINGS
TO OOR HEELS."

MASTER GALT, THE ERRAND BOY.

SIR ALEX. GALT, who occupied the position of Canadian High Commissioner in England, returned to Canada at this time. It was believed that he had been summoned by the Government, but the nature of his business was not made known.

GRIP, OCTOBER 11th, 1879.

MASTER GALT, THE NEW ERRAND BOY.

SIR JOHN.—"WELL, DID YOU DELIVER MY MESSAGE ABOUT THE TARIFF TO MR. BULL?"

MASTER GALT.—"YES, I TOLD HIM IT WAS A REVENUE TARIFF."

SIR JOHN.—"AND WHAT DID HE SAY?"

MASTER GALT.—"HE ONLY LAUGHED."

THE MODERN NERO.

THE *Globe* published, with every appearance of glee, a statement showing an increase in the mercantile failures in Canada for the current year.

GRIP, JANUARY 24th, 1880.

BUSINESS
FAILURES
1879,
(FIRST YEAR OF THE N.P.)
1,902,
$29,347,937.

MACKENZIE'S
REGIME.

1875 - 1968 FAILURES, $28,843,467
1876 - 1728   "   25,517,991.
1877 - 1892   "   25,523,903
1878 - 1697   "   23,908,677

$503,970 LESS
THAN THE
FIRST YEAR OF THE
N P

THE MODERN NERO.

FIDDLING AT THE DESTRUCTION OF CANADIAN COMMERCE.

A BIT OF FATHERLY ADVICE.

ON Tuesday, 27th April, Mr. Blake formally assumed the leadership of the Reform Party as successor to Hon. Mr. Mackenzie.

GRIP, MAY 8th, 1880.

A BIT OF FATHERLY ADVICE.

SIR JOHN.—"NOW, EDWARD, BE STEADY, SOBER, STRAIGHTFORWARD, AND KEEP YOUR HANDS CLEAN, AND YOU
MAY BECOME AS GREAT A SUCCESS AS I AM."

THE ANNUAL BLOW-OUT.

ONE of the chief arguments used by the Government in support of their establishment of a Canadian High Commissioner in England, was that that functionary would attend to the business which heretofore had necessitated frequent visits by Ministers. Although the occupant of the office, at this date, Sir Alexander Galt, was admittedly a most competent man, the customary summer trip on public business was made by no fewer than three Members of the Cabinet—Sir John Macdonald, Sir Charles Tupper, and Hon. H. W. Pope.

GRIP, JULY 17th, 1880.

THE ANNUAL BLOW-OUT!

SIR A. T. GALT.—"WHAT, YOU HERE PERSONALLY; AM *I* NOT, THEN, CAPABLE OF TRANSACTING THE BUSINESS
OF THE DOMINION AS HIGH COMMISSIONER?"

SIR JOHN—"THE BUSINESS? OH, CERTAINLY; BUT WE COULDN'T HAVE OUR ANNUAL JUNKETING BY *PROXY*,
YOU KNOW."

THE CANADIAN GANGES.

THE business upon which the ministers had gone to England pertained to the building of the C. P. Ry., and statements were received in Canada which gave rise to the fear that a bargain would be concluded which would lead to vast monopoly evils.

GRIP, JULY 24th, 1880.

THE CANADIAN GANGES; OR, THE CONTEMPLATED SACRIFICE.

ALL OFF ONE LAST.

In arranging the new tariff no discrimination was made in favor of British goods.   This display of " even handed justice " on the part of the Canadian Government called forth a good deal of criticism from the English papers.

Grip, August 14th, 1880.

ALL OFF THE ONE LAST!

JOHN A. (N. P. SHOEMAKER).—"PINCH, DO THEY? OF COURSE; WE MAKE 'EM TO PINCH. LOOK AT THAT YANKEE
CHAP! HOWEVER, WE DON'T MIND STRETCHING 'EM *A LEETLE* TO ACCOMMODATE A RELATIVE LIKE *YOU*."

ALE FELLOW, WELL MET!

SIR LEONARD TILLEY, who as a Member of the Cabinet represented the Temperance element, and had long been a leader in one of the prominent Teetotal orders, scandalized his friends throughout the country by delivering a speech at a brewery in Dartmouth, N.S., in which he congratulated the proprietors on their prosperity, and expressed the hope that the business might still further succeed. It need scarcely be said that, at the moment, Sir Leonard was speaking in his political capacity—as the author of the N. P., which had so greatly assisted the brewing industry.

GRIP, SEPTEMBER 25th, 1880.

'ALE FELLOW, WELL MET!

"HE TRUSTED THAT THE BUSINESS WOULD SO CONTINUE TO INCREASE THAT THE PROPRIETORS WOULD FIND
THEMSELVES CRAMPED FOR ROOM, AND BE OBLIGED, IN CONSEQUENCE, TO EXTEND THEIR QUARTERS."

[SIR S. L. TILLEY'S SPEECH AT OLANDS & CO.'S BREWERY, DARTMOUTH, N.S., REPORTED IN THE "HERALD" (CONSERVATIVE).]

A PIG IN A POKE.

VERY great curiosity was manifested by the Opposition press to learn the nature of the bargain which had been made for the building of the Canadian Pacific Railway, and which, according to a public statement of Sir John Macdonald, "would not cost the country a cent in cash."

GRIP, NOVEMBER 13th, 1880.

"A PIG IN A POKE."

MASTER BUNTING.—"IT'S A SPLENDID PIG, I TELL YOU; AND IF YOU SAY IT ISN'T, I'LL SMACK YER ACROSS THE
   SNOOT."
MASTER BROWN.—"I DON'T SAY NOTHIN' ABOUT IT; I ONLY WANT TO *SEE* THE ANIMAL, THAT'S ALL!"

THE SYNDICATE CHRISTMAS TREE.

THE terms of the bargain were such as to create profound astonishment throughout the country.   Aside from enormous subsidies in money and land (representing some $50,000,000), the Bill conferred franchises and monopolies upon the contracting company that were most dangerous and extravagant.

GRIP, DECEMBER 25th, 1880.

THE SYNDICATE'S CHRISTMAS TREE;

OR, THE TIME FOR GIVING THINGS AWAY.

TAKING THE BULL BY THE HORNS.

THE numerous amendments moved by members of the Opposition during the discussion of the Railway Bill were voted down by a majority which worked with all the perfection of a marionette.

GRIP, JANUARY 29th, 1881.

"TAKING THE BULL BY THE HORNS;"

OR, THE "NOBLE ATTITUDE" OF THE OPPOSITION.

THE CONTRACT SWALLOWED.

―――――――――

THAT this outrageous bargain should have been ratified after full discussion of its details, and in the presence of a *bona fide* offer of equally competent contractors to build the road at vastly less cost, was another striking illustration of the swallowing capacity of Canadian partyism.

GRIP, FEBRUARY 19th, 1881.

THE CONTRACT SWALLOWED.

SIR JOHN.—"YES, IT'S DOWN, SURE ENOUGH; BUT I'M AFRAID IT WON'T DIGEST."

MISS CANADA'S SURPLUS.

THE Government boasted of a large surplus of revenue, and paid no attention to the carping critics who kept reminding them that a large surplus
simply meant an unnecessary bleeding of the tax-payer.

GRIP, SEPTEMBER 10th, 1881.

MISS CANADA'S SURPLUS.

LANGEVIN (Doctor's Assistant).—"SEE, MADAME, OUR LEECH HAS DRAWN A GREAT SURPLUS OF BLOOD FROM
YOU; YOU MUST BE GROWING STRONGER."

THE PACIFIC YOUNGSTER PACIFIED.

SIR CHARLES TUPPER, Minister of Railways, paid a visit to British Columbia, and to all appearance was successful in his efforts to convince the people of that Province of the good intentions of the Government. A want of confidence had been the prevailing feeling there ever since the inauguration of the Railway scheme of the Reform Government.

GRIP, SEPTEMBER 17th, 1881.

THE PACIFIC YOUNGSTER PACIFIED.

SIR CHARLES.—"WELL, THEN, AND DID HIS BAD, BAD MACKENZIE MAKE A FOOLEY TOOLEY OF HIM, SO HE
DID; BUT HE SHALL HAVE HIS ISLAND RAILWAY, SO HE SHALL; AND HE'LL ALWAYS VOTE FOR HIS
SIR CHARLEY, SO HE SHALL!"

THE AID OF A GLASS.

Sir John Macdonald had made very extravagant promises as to the marvels which the N. P. would produce in the way of factories, etc., etc. As these glowing views failed of anything like full realization, the ante-election statements were a favorite morsel with the *Globe* and other Opposition papers.

Grip, October 15th, 1881.

THE AID OF A GLASS!

GORDON B.—"AH! YOU'RE RIGHT, SIR JOHN; LOOKING THROUGH *THIS* MEDIUM I DO SEE FACTORY CHIMNEYS
IN EVERY TOWN AND VILLAGE IN THE COUNTRY."

THAT TROUBLESOME YOUNGSTER.

THE C. P. R. Syndicate next threw out hints that it would be pleased to possess itself of the timber along the line east of Winnipeg. This property, according to the decision of the Boundary Commission, belonged to Ontario.

GRIP, NOVEMBER 5th, 1881.

THAT TROUBLESOME YOUNGSTER.

INDULGENT MAMMA MACDONALD.—"IT MUST BE A GOOD LITTLE MONOPOLY, AND IT MUSN'T CRY FOR OLIVER'S THINGS, OR MAMMA 'LL HAVE TO——"

SPINSTER BLAKE (SOTTO VOCE).—"OH, IF *I* ONLY HAD THE MANAGEMENT OF THAT CHE-ILD!"

THE (RAIL) "ROAD AGENT."

THE Dominion Government intimated their intention of disallowing a charter granted by the Legislature of Manitoba for the construction of a line competing with the St. Paul, Minnesota and Manitoba Railroad, within the boundaries of that Province.   Dr. Schultz, M.P., was a prominent promoter of the proposed line.

GRIP, NOVEMBER 19th, 1881.

THE (RAIL) "ROAD AGENT."

HOW LONG WILL THE PEOPLE OF THE DOMINION SUBMIT TO THIS INSOLENT HIGHWAYMAN?

CENTRALIZATION.

———————

THE action of the Dominion Government in the matter of the Manitoba charters, taken in connection with similar interferences with the rights of other Provinces, revived the recollection that Sir John Macdonald had opposed the Federal system, and pronounced in favor of a Legislative union, prior to 1867.

GRIP, FEBRUARY 11th, 1882.

"CENTRALIZATION;"
OR, "PROVINCIAL AUTONOMY ABOLISHED."
IS THIS WHAT SIR JOHN IS AIMING AT?

MISS CANADA VACCINATED.

———————

THE worst consequences were predicted by the Opposition leaders to result from the monopoly granted to the C.P.R. Co. Mr. Blake, however, gave expression to no plan by which, if entrusted with the case, he could hope to avert the danger.

GRIP, FEBRUARY 25th, 1882.

MISS CANADA VACCINATED.

DR. JOHN A.—"AH, MADAM, IT IS TAKING SPLENDIDLY!"

DR. BLAKE.—"YES, LOOKS AS THOUGH IT WOULD END *FATALLY.* MADAM, DISMISS THAT QUACK, AND TAKE ME ON."

MISS CANADA.—"AND WHAT WOULD YOU DO IN THE CASE?"

DR. BLAKE.—"I WOULD—UM—ER—OCCUPY HIS POSITION."

THE FIFTH WHEEL.

DISCUSSION was again rife as to the uselessness and expensiveness of the Dominion Senate.

GRIP, APRIL 8th, 1882.

THE FIFTH WHEEL TO OUR GOVERNMENT COACH.

THE GRIT NURSERY.

———————

Sir John Macdonald was credited with the statement that one of the objects of the Redistribution Bill was to "hive the Grits." This the measure most effectually did, in many instances.

Grip, May 20th, 1882.

THE GRIT NURSERY.

TROUBLED WITH "HIVES."

A GLORIOUS PROSPECT.

WHILE the tariff proved a decided boon to manufacturers in some branches, there was no general rise in wages to correspond to the increase in the cost of living.

GRIP, JUNE 10th, 1882.

A GLORIOUS PROSPECT.

THE AULD WOMAN.—"TRULY, AS YOU SAY, SIR, THE PASTURE IS VERA POOR, BUT THE COW HAS A GRAND VIEW!"

LET THE BIG CHIEF BEWARE.

THE high handed conduct of the Dominion Government towards Manitoba, in disallowing her railway charters, etc., excited much opposition in that Province against Sir John Macdonald.

GRIP, NOVEMBER 18th, 1882.

LET THE BIG CHIEF BEWARE!

SIR JOHN SURRENDERS HIS SWORD.

SEVERAL injurious amendments were made in the Canada Temperance Act in its passage through Committee of the Whole. These changes were in the interests of the liquor traffic, which was represented in the Cabinet by Hon. John Carling.

GRIP, MAY 26th, 1883.

SIR JOHN SURRENDERS HIS SWORD.

A LITTLE TOO MUCH OF THE WHIP.

THE Federal Government continued from time to time to manifest a dispo-
sition to encroach upon the rights reserved to the Provinces under the
British North America Act.   For prudential reasons, however, Quebec was
interfered with less than the others.

GRIP, JUNE 16th, 1883.

A LITTLE TOO MUCH OF THE WHIP.

DUNDREARY'S "WIDDLE."

THE C. P. R. Syndicate asked for and received a Government guarantee of three per cent. for ten years on $100,000,000 worth of its stock. There was much mystery as usual about this arrangement, but the fact that it was carried through quite readily by the Government proved that the Company's power of securing favors was practically unlimited.

GRIP, NOVEMBER 10th, 1883.

DUNDREARY'S "WIDDLE!"

"WH-WHY DOES THE D-DOG WAGGLE THE T-TAIL? BECAUSE THE D-DOG IS STRONGER THAN THE T-TAIL—
OTHERWISE THE T-TAIL WOULD WAG-WAGGLE THE D-DOG!"

MACPHERSON'S OPPORTUNITY.

THE North-West land policy persisted in by the Canadian Government was having the effect of driving Canadian settlers into the American territories where the regulations were more liberal.

GRIP, NOVEMBER 17th, 1883.

MR. MACPHERSON'S OPPORTUNITY.

A GRAND CHANCE FOR THE MINISTER OF THE INTERIOR TO WIN CANADA'S GRATITUDE.

MERELY A HUM-BUG-BEAR.

A DESPATCH from the North-West, published in the *Globe*, intimated that trouble was brewing amongst the settlers in that distant part of the country, and that unless action was at once taken to redress the grievances complained of, open rebellion might result. This report was pronounced by the *Mail* to be untruthful, and to be merely the result of a "bear" movement to depress Canada Pacific stock on the market.

GRIP, NOVEMBER 24th, 1883.

MERELY A HUM-BUG-BEAR!

THE EDITOR OF THE *MAIL* NOT A BIT SCARED.